Movements in Art **LATE MODERNISM**

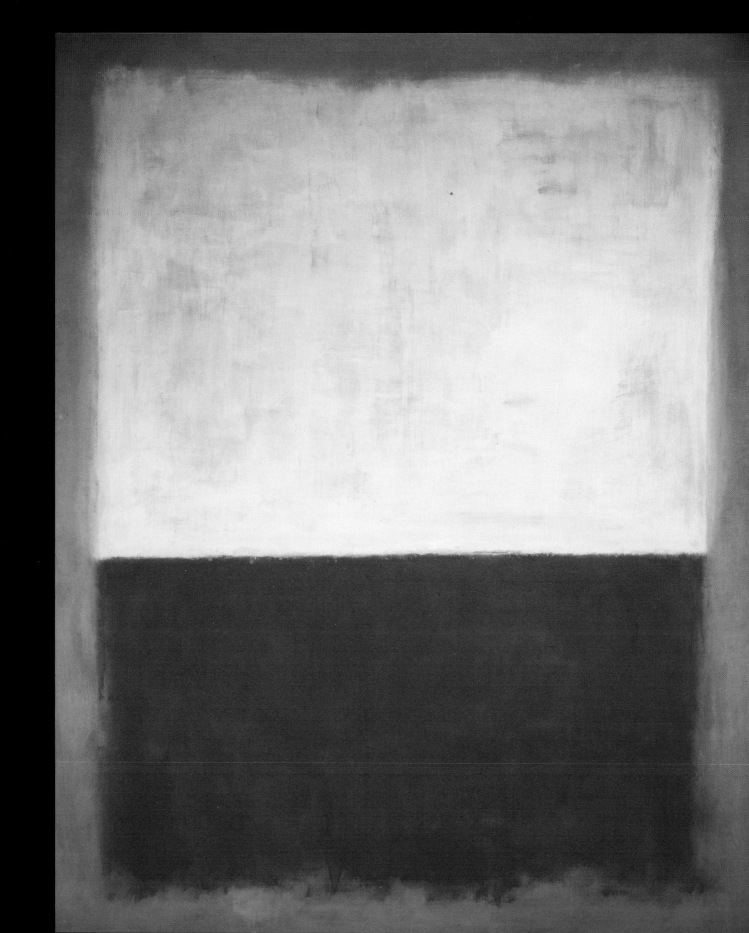

Movements in Art **LATE MODERNISM**

ANNE FITZPATRICK

CREATIVE EDUCATION

Published by Creative Education
123 South Broad Street, Mankato, Minnesota 56001
Creative Education is an imprint of The Creative Company

Design and production by Blue Design (www.bluedes.com)
Art direction by Rita Marshall

Photographs by Art Resource, NY (The Andy Warhol Foundation, Inc.,
CNAC/MNAM/Dist. Réunion des Musées Nationaux, The Museum of
Modern Art/Licensed by SCALA, National Portrait Gallery, Smithsonian
Institution, The Philadelphia Museum of Art, Smithsonian American Art
Museum, Washington, DC, Tate Gallery, London), Corbis (Andy Warhol
Foundation, Bettmann, Burstein Collection, Geoffrey Clements, Christopher
Felver, Allen Ginsberg, Robert Holmes, DOUG KUNTZ/CORBIS SYGMA,
Michael Nicholson, Shepard Sherbell, Scott T. Smith, Lee Snider/Photo Im-
ages, Underwood & Underwood, Roger Wood)

Library of Congress Cataloging-in-Publication Data

Fitzpatrick, Anne, 1978–
Late modernism / by Anne Fitzpatrick.
p. cm. — (Movements in art)
ISBN 978-1-58341-348-7
1. Modernism (Art)—United States—Juvenile literature. 2. Art, American—
20th century—Juvenile literature. I. Title. II. Series.

N6512.5.M63F57 2004
709'.73'09045—dc22   2004056166

9 8 7 6 5 4 3 2

Cover: Brushstroke by Roy Lichtenstein (1965)
Page 2: No. 12 by Mark Rothko (1954)
Pages 4–5: Booster from the series "Booster and the 7 Studies" by Robert
  Rauschenberg (1967)

Late Modernism

The history of the world can be told through accounts of great battles, the lives of kings and queens, and the discoveries and inventions of scientists and explorers. But the history of the way people think and feel about themselves and the world is told through art. From paintings of the hunt in prehistoric caves, to sacred art in the European Middle Ages, to the abstract forms of the 20th century, movements in art are the expression of a culture. Sometimes that expression is so powerful and compelling that it reaches through time to carry its message to another generation.

From an abstract painting (opposite) by Willem de Kooning to Andy Warhol's *Campbell's Soup Can (Tomato)* **(1965, above), Late Modernism encompasses a variety of subjects, artists, styles, and modes of expression.**

Toward the end of the 19th century, artists began to talk about the need for "modern" art. As traditional forms of society, such as rigid class structures and powerful religious ties, disappeared, a new world was emerging. The Modernist art movement sought a new art to express it. But the world was changing so quickly that artists never felt that they had caught up. More than 50 years after Modernism began, the artists of Late Modernism were still trying to cope with the feeling that everything had changed. That feeling and the diverse ways they found to express it continue to resonate in today's fast-paced world.

THE AMERICAN CENTURY

From 1939 to 1945, most of the world was at war. Germany, led by Adolf Hitler and his National Socialist (Nazi) party, invaded and occupied much of Europe. A group of allied nations led by Great Britain, the United States, the **U.S.S.R.**, and France fought back and eventually succeeded in containing and defeating Germany. Meanwhile, Japan took advantage of the distraction in Europe to invade China. After five years of war in the Pacific, the U.S. forced Japan to surrender by dropping the first atomic bombs on two of its major cities, Hiroshima

THE ATOMIC AGE

Atomic, or nuclear, bombs harness the energy released when an atom (one of the tiny building blocks that make up all matter) is split. They were dropped on Hiroshima and Nagasaki, Japan, in 1945, the first and last times that atomic weapons have ever been used. Nearly 66,000 people in Hiroshima and 39,000 in Nagasaki were killed the moment the bombs exploded, and the harmful radiation released by the explosions sickened thousands more. The immense devastation caused by the bombs horrified the world. Atomic bombs continued to be built, but they became a weapon of diplomacy; no one wanted to risk starting a war in which such weapons would be used.

By the end of World War II, more than 90 percent of the city center of Cologne, Germany, had been destroyed, and many other urban centers in the country had been reduced to rubble.

and Nagasaki. World War II, as the conflicts became known, affected more people and caused more sweeping changes than any other war in history.

When the war finally ended, Europe was in ruins, and nearly 15 million Europeans were dead. Housing, factories, roads, and communication systems had been destroyed. It would be decades before the European **economy** would recover. The U.S. and the U.S.S.R. were the only two great powers left in the world. The war had actually benefited them, expanding the U.S.S.R.'s territory in Europe and pulling American industries out of the Great Depression—the economic slump of the 1930s. By 1947, the U.S. was the wealthiest nation in the world; it produced nearly 60 percent of the world's steel and manufactured more than 80 percent of the world's automobiles. Many proclaimed the arrival of "The American Century."

With the need to cooperate against Germany and Japan gone, the U.S.S.R. suddenly seemed threatening to the U.S. In the years that followed the war, the world began to be divided between **Communist** nations under the influence of the U.S.S.R. and countries allied with the U.S. Because the tension that continued for the next four decades never escalated into actual war, it was known as the "Cold War." The fact that both the U.S. and the U.S.S.R. had atomic weapons made their mutual hostility particularly ominous; fear of atomic warfare cast a dark shadow over global politics. In the U.S., there was pressure to conform to a set idea of what it meant to be American, and people who seemed to sympathize with the Communists were persecuted.

World War II and its aftermath had a profound effect on art. Death and destruction on such a massive scale, the horrors of the **Holocaust**, and the oppressive atmosphere of the Cold War left artists reeling with questions

THE RED THREAT AND McCARTHYISM

Cold War **propaganda** taught Americans to live in fear of "The Red Threat"—the possibility that American workers might start their own Communist revolution and raise the U.S.S.R.'s red flag on American soil. In 1950, Senator Joseph McCarthy announced that more than 200 "card-carrying Communists"

had infiltrated the U.S. government. Although he could not name a single Communist or provide any proof, the anxious nation was willing to believe it. As the chairman of a newly created "Un-American Activities Committee," Senator McCarthy led a witch hunt for Communist sympathizers, questioning thousands of people. No one was ever charged, but the suspicion was enough to ruin people's lives. The wave of unfounded persecution became known as "McCarthyism."

Some of the greatest artists in Russia were put to work creating propaganda posters during the Russian Revolution. This political poster from around 1917 features an Uncle Sam-like figure saying, "You—Still Not a Member of the Cooperative, Sign up Immediately!"

about the purpose and relevance of art. During the Great Depression, artists had created art with a message; they believed in their ability to inspire social reform through paintings of people working together for a better society. After the war, artists were disillusioned and pessimistic. If, as the war made it seem, human beings were essentially irrational and evil, it was useless to try to appeal to them through art. The use of art as propaganda by the governments of Nazi Germany and Communist Russia also made such efforts seem illegitimate and suspicious.

In New York, a group of artists concluded that the only purpose of making art should be making art. They rejected the idea that art needed to have any outside value, whether from politics, morality, or beauty. Instead, art was an expression of the artist's individuality and creativity—a defiant slap at the oppressive conformity of 1950s America. They produced art that had little or no reference to a reality outside itself. The violent, rhythmic paint splatters of Jackson Pollock (1912–56) and the vivid, intense color blocks of Mark Rothko (1903–70) reflected only the inner reality of the artist. By 1950, these Abstract Expressionists, as they became known, dominated the art world. American artists had always followed the lead of European artists, but now, for the first time, they created their own artistic style. As the Late Modernist period began, New York replaced Paris, France, as the capital city of Western art.

Life moved faster in the 20th century than in earlier times. Art movements such as the Renaissance were dominated by a unified, distinctive style that lasted more than 100 years, but the Late Modernist movement was a collection of smaller movements. Their styles were often dissimilar,

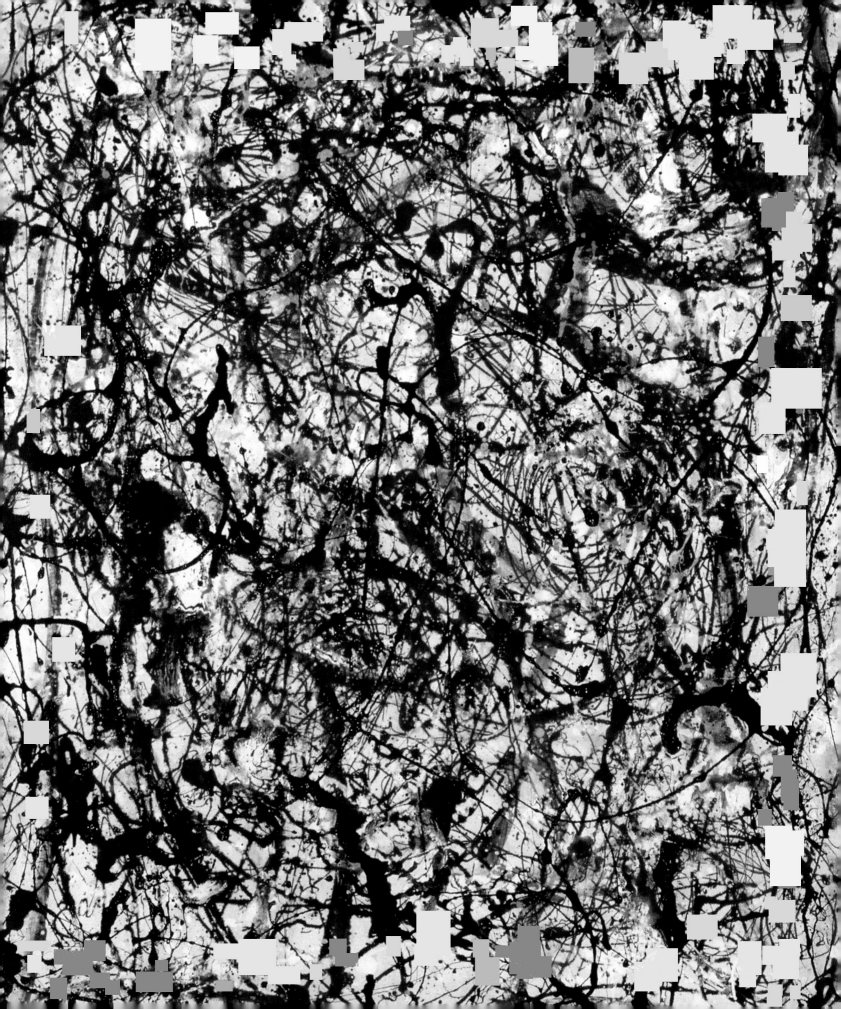

THE BEAT GENERATION

A rebellious strain of youth culture brought a breath of fresh air into the repressive conformity of 1950s America. Members of the Beat movement were disillusioned and worn out—"beat"—by what they perceived as the emptiness of modern life. They gathered in New York's Greenwich Village and the North Beach neighborhood of San Francisco to listen to the music of Charlie Parker, Dizzy Gillespie, and Miles Davis and discuss radical political ideas. The free-form, spontaneous writing of novelists Jack Kerouac and Edgar Rice Burroughs and poet Allen Ginsburg became the voice of the Beat generation, verbalizing their alienation and frustration. (Pictured: Miles Davis, left, and Charlie Parker, below)

although they were reacting to similar events and influences. A new generation of artists was challenging the ideas of Abstract Expressionism within 10 years. Abstract Expressionist art was focused inward, removed from the real world, and was often difficult for viewers to understand and engage with. Many artists reacted to it by setting out to reconnect art and life, and to make art more accessible for the public.

The Neo-Dada movement (named after Dada, an art movement that took place in France from about 1915 to 1925) that rose to challenge Abstract Expressionism during the 1950s used or depicted ordinary objects in **collages**, sculptures, and paintings. By making art with objects that had been created in factories, such artists as Robert Rauschenberg (1925–) and Jasper Johns (1930–) denied the Abstract Expressionist claim that art should be solely the expression of the artist's individuality. They were also making a statement about the **commercialization** of art. The art world was increasingly dominated by private art galleries in which the art being exhibited was also for sale, and many felt this made art less "pure."

Some artists tried to avoid commercialization by creating art that could not be sold. They organized events called "happenings," during which they might wear strange costumes, read aloud, play music, act out scenes, or dance. Such art events disappeared as soon as they were created, leaving nothing to be bought and sold. In one happening, artist Jean Tinguely (1925–91) set fire to his sculpture *Homage to New York* (1960) while an invited audience watched and cheered. Often the audience at happenings was invited to participate, breaking down the traditional barrier between art and the viewer. In *GAS* (1966), Allen Kaprow (1927–) invited people to parks in several American

Although he studied art in Paris, Robert Rauschenberg soon found himself disillusioned with the European art scene. He moved back to the United States, where he began an artistic revolution, focusing on new mediums such as collage and "combines," three-dimensional works that combined various objects from the everyday world.

Andy Warhol transformed contemporary art through both his subject matter and techniques. This self-portrait (below) from 1986 is one of many he made throughout his life, experimenting with different poses, expressions, and mediums.

cities and provided them with objects such as steel barrels and large, gas-filled balloons. As they moved the objects around, the constantly changing scene became a temporary work of art.

The commercialization of art was part of a larger trend. Western society was increasingly focused on possessing and consuming goods. Television and other media were becoming ever-present, and they flooded the public with advertising. Pop Art, a movement that grew out of Neo-Dada during the 1960s, embraced this commercialization of culture. Artists such as Roy Lichtenstein (1923–97) and Andy Warhol (1928–87) used the images of advertising and popular entertainment to reflect everyday life. They manipulated the instantly recognizable symbolism of such images to create **ironic** commentaries on contemporary life, culture, and politics. Some artists and art **critics** proclaimed that it was the death of art—just as they had when Abstract Expressionists first appeared—but Pop Art, like Abstract Expressionism, soon became wildly popular.

LATE MODERN ARTISTS

During World War II, a community of artists developed in Greenwich Village, a neighborhood of New York. They formed discussion groups, established art schools, and published magazines to spread their views on art. Mark Rothko was an important part of this fertile art scene, although his fellow artists gave him a hard time for being so serious

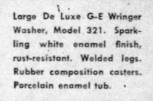

THE NEW CULTURE OF CONSUMERISM

In the years after World War II, improvements in industry and technology contributed to a booming economy and growing middle class. The number and variety of goods available increased at the same time that more Americans could better afford to buy them. Americans rushed to own new washing machines, vacuum cleaners, radios, TVs, ste-

reos, and other gadgets. With their retirement income assured by a new social security program, they were less worried about saving and more willing to go into debt. Credit card use exploded. Advertising was also on the rise, promoting the new products and enticing eager consumers. Shopping was no longer just another household chore—it was fun for the whole family.

Although much of his art was abstract, Mark Rothko paid close attention to formal artistic elements such as color, shape, balance, depth, composition, and scale, yet at the same time refused to provide any explanation of his works.

about his artistic ambitions. Rothko's strict, traditional Jewish family had emigrated from Russia to settle in Portland, Oregon, when he was 10 years old. The family was very poor throughout his childhood and adolescence. After moving to New York in 1923, Rothko studied art and became an art teacher, struggling to make ends meet. He lived in a tiny apartment near the Museum of Modern Art, which he often visited.

Rothko's style evolved slowly over the next 20 years. He began to feel that portraying the forms and figures of reality was inadequate for true artistic expression. Figures, he thought, were "obstacles between the painter and the idea and between the idea and the observer." By 1947, his paintings had become completely **abstract**. But they were not paintings about nothing, Rothko was quick to point out. He strove to express human emotions and the tragedy of human existence. Rothko thought of his paintings as a religious experience; he made them on a large scale so that the viewer would be enveloped by them, creating an intense intimacy. His ideas were radical, and many people found the paintings difficult to understand and appreciate. But by the time of his death in 1970, Rothko's distinctive style was recognized and admired throughout the world.

Jackson Pollock was another important member of the Greenwich Village art scene, where he was known for his moodiness and arrogance. He grew up in Wyoming, Arizona, and California amid wide open spaces and Native American culture, which would be important influences on his work. At age 18, he followed his brother Sande to New York to become an artist. They studied with Thomas Hart Benton (1889–1975), who was painting colorful scenes of American life. Pollock copied his style but injected a sense of move-

PLACE TO VISIT: MUSEUM OF MODERN ART, NEW YORK

The Museum of Modern Art (MOMA) in New York contains more than 135,000 paintings, sculptures, photographs, and other objects of art. MOMA's collection includes such masterpieces of Late Modernism as Jackson Pollock's *One* (1950), Jasper Johns's *Flag*, Andy Warhol's *Gold Marilyn Monroe* (1962), Willem de Kooning's *Seated Woman* (1952), and Roy Lichtenstein's *Drowning Girl* (1963). The original six-story building, completed in 1939, was recently reno-

vated to double the exhibition space and create light, airy **galleries** overlooking the outdoor sculpture garden, which was designed in 1953. A few subway stops away, one can explore the art galleries, shops, and parks of Greenwich Village, once home to the Abstract Expressionists.

PLACE TO VISIT: KRASNER-POLLOCK HOUSE AND STUDIO, LONG ISLAND

From 1946 until Jackson Pollock's death in 1956, he and his wife Lee Krasner lived in a house on Long Island, off the coast of New York. The house has been preserved as a museum and is open to the public for guided tours. Their furniture and personal possessions remain in the house,

which looks much as it did when they lived there. In the converted barn that Pollock used as a **studio**, the floor is so spattered with paint that it looks like one of his paintings. The brushes and other working materials of both artists are on display, as well as family snapshots that offer an intimate glimpse into the artists' lives.

ment and mystery that was his own. Gradually those elements took over, and recognizable figures began to disappear from his paintings.

In about 1947, Pollock began pouring paint directly from the can onto canvas laid on the floor. He spattered and dripped dense layers of paint rhythmically across the whole length and width of canvases that were often as tall as 7 feet (2 m) and as long as 16 feet (5 m). Many people wondered how such "accidental" creations could be called art. In 1949, *Life* magazine called Pollock "the greatest living painter in the United States." But his work continued to be **controversial**, and Pollock's lifelong struggles with alcoholism and depression worsened as his fame grew. His wife, artist Lee Krasner (1908–84), left him in 1956. A few months later, he was killed in an automobile accident.

Willem de Kooning (1904–97) became a part of the artists' community in Greenwich Village when he arrived in the United States as a stowaway on a ship. De Kooning grew up in Holland, where he trained as a commercial artist by day and attended fine arts classes at night. When he was 22, he left for America to seek his fortune. He found work painting houses and signs in New York. It was not until 1948, when he had his first **one-man show**, that his art began attracting attention. De Kooning's bold, abstract black-and-white paintings drew favorable reviews from critics. But in 1950, de Kooning suddenly abandoned the abstract style that had launched his career and began working on a series of paintings of women. Many critics and fellow artists were horrified at this return to depicting figures.

De Kooning's paintings of women continue to be controversial today, but for a different reason: the violent, even frightening, depictions, in which the

Throughout his artistic career, Willem de Kooning revisited the theme of the female figure often, producing much-talked-about paintings, including *Woman Seated III*, the meaning and intention of which are still disputed.

female figures appear to be on the verge of destruction or disintegration, are often seen as part of a **misogynist** current in Abstract Expressionism. De Kooning had a strained relationship with his wife, Elaine Fried de Kooning. Like Pollock's wife Lee Krasner, Elaine was an artist whose work was always perceived in the shadow of her husband's larger fame. Abstract Expressionism celebrated the artist as "tough guy," idealizing a brooding, threatening figure who expressed his inner violence through art. This emphasis on masculinity made it difficult for female artists to gain recognition.

Although de Kooning's women were regarded by many as a shocking return to depicting reality, they continued Abstract Expressionism's emphasis on expressing the inner turmoil of the artist. It would take a new artistic movement to turn art's gaze outward again. Jasper Johns and Robert Rauschenberg lived and worked in New York in the 1940s and '50s but stayed away from the Greenwich Village community. Rauschenberg, who was born in a small town in Texas, created collages and sculptures with items such as postcards, tires, toothpaste, bed linen, and a stuffed rooster. Johns, who grew up in South Carolina, made large, colorful paintings of instantly recognizable objects such as targets and American flags.

The two friends gained fame in 1958 after a gallery owner, invited by Rauschenberg to their shared studio, was fascinated by Johns's work and gave him his own show—soon followed by a one-man show for Rauschenberg. Although the shows made them celebrities, not everyone was a fan; one critic called the award of a major art prize to Rauschenberg "the total and general defeat of culture," and an artist at Johns's show said, "If this is painting, I might as well give up."

Despite the controversy some of his works caused, other of de Kooning's pieces were highly sought after. His *Pink Lady* (1944) sold for $3.6 million in 1987, while *Interchange* (1955) brought in $20.6 million two years later. Alzheimer's disease forced de Kooning to stop painting around 1990.

PLACE TO VISIT: THE WARHOL MUSEUM, PITTSBURGH

Located in Pittsburgh, Pennsylvania, near Warhol's hometown, the Andy Warhol Museum is the most comprehensive single-artist museum in the world. More than 4,000 works of art are collected there, including paintings, drawings, prints, photographs, sculpture, film, and other records and documents relating to the artist. The museum theater shows his films and episodes of his cable television shows "Andy Warhol's TV," "Andy Warhol's Fifteen Minutes," and "Factory Diaries." Warhol's student work and commercial art are displayed, as well as the paintings that made him famous. Special exhibitions focus on specific areas of his work or related artists such as Warhol's protégé Jean-Michel Basquiat (1960–88). (Pictured: *Flowers*, 1964, by Andy Warhol)

Repetition was key to many of Warhol's works, including *One Hundred Campbell's Soup Cans* (1962), which focuses on the sameness of the cans to imitate and comment on the conditions of mass advertising.

The work of Rauschenberg and Johns prepared the way for the emergence of Pop Art, a movement that bridged the gap between art and life so completely that its masterpieces are often indistinguishable from the imagery of advertising and entertainment. Pop artist Roy Lichtenstein found his signature style when his young son pointed to a Mickey Mouse comic book and said, "I bet you can't paint as good as that." The artist worked painstakingly to disguise his brush strokes and recreate the clean lines of comic book images. He used **stencils** to make rows of identical dots that mimicked comics' printing processes. When he took the first six comic book paintings to a New York gallery, they were immediately accepted for exhibition.

Lichtenstein was born in New York but studied art at Ohio State University. He was drafted in 1943 and fought in Europe during World War II. He worked for years in various styles without success until his son suggested comic books. Although the paintings brought him attention and recognition, many people were shocked to see comics on gallery walls. A 1964 article in *Life* magazine asked, "Is He the Worst Artist in the U.S.?" But eventually, the easy appeal of his paintings made them more widely popular.

Pop Art's best-known celebrity, Andy Warhol, began his career as an award-winning designer of advertising. Born to Czechoslovakian immigrants in Pennsylvania, Warhol made his way to New York after college, intent on creating great art. His main artistic goal was to get people to stop and look at something that would otherwise go unnoticed amid the constant bombardment of advertising and media. Inspired by a friend's joke, he began making paintings of Campbell's soup cans, experimenting with commercial methods such as **silk-screening** to achieve a factory-made appearance.

Created after the movie star's death, Warhol's brightly colored *Marilyn Monroe (Marilyn)* (1967, opposite) is one of several images the artist made of celebrities and is an example of his use of the silk-screening technique. *Mineola Motorcycle* (c. 1985–86, left) illustrates Warhol's unique use of advertising imagery in his art.

The Campbell's soup can paintings were a sensation at a 1962 show. Suddenly famous, Warhol founded a studio in New York named, ironically, "The Factory," where he and a team of young artists churned out artwork in astonishing quantities. Warhol led a wild, eccentric life, surrounding himself with beautiful, interesting people. He thought of himself as a brand name or designer label, and his life, appearance, and personality were as much a part of his artwork as the paint and canvas. Nor was he shy about treating his art as a business—for example, he painted portraits of wealthy businessmen and gave them discounts for buying large quantities. Warhol embraced the new influences that others feared would be the death of art, using them to inject a new vitality into the art world.

GREAT WORKS OF LATE MODERNISM

Architecture became more expressive and flexible during the postwar period, breaking from the straight lines and austere spaces of late 19th- and early 20th-century "Rationalist" architecture. One of the last buildings by architect Frank Lloyd Wright (1867–1959), who had begun challenging Rationalist ideas as early as 1908, was a museum of abstract art, the Solomon R. Guggenheim Museum

(1943–59) in New York. His design drew on Native American architecture and the grand, curving lines of the Grand Canyon. Most of the building's interior consists of a skylit spiral ramp. Visitors take an elevator to the top of the building and stroll down, for a fluid and intimate museum experience. Wright's organic style was very influential for Late Modern architects. For example, the TWA Terminal (1956–62) at New York's John F. Kennedy Airport, designed in 1956 by Finnish architect Eero Saarinen (1910–61), is a dazzling intersection of curving lines that create a feeling of movement. The building almost looks like a giant bird spreading its wings.

Movement is the central feeling evoked by Pollock's *Autumn Rhythm: Number 30* (1950). The painting is typical of the art he created between 1947 and 1951, launching his career and the Abstract Expressionist movement.

Although Pollock left large gaps of raw canvas exposed and used only black and white paint, the result is powerful. Violent slashes of paint point in every direction, spattered by drips and blots. The viewer is invited to imagine the artist at work, throwing paint at the canvas frantically, perhaps in rage. It is not an easy painting to view. There is no place where the eye may rest; it is drawn from one place to another by the lines of paint, pulled into the depths of layered paint only to be pushed out again by the smooth surface of unpainted canvas. One feels lost, even trapped, and shares the painter's frustration.

Pollock's tensions and violence are a sharp contrast to the placid depths of Rothko's paintings, such as *Untitled* (1951). The soft edges of the blocks of color give them the appearance of floating, and subtle variations of shade create a sense of depth. The colors chosen for the two largest sections, red and green, are in perfect harmony, setting off and complementing each other. The immense serenity of the painting, uncomplicated by distracting figures, gently leads the viewer toward contemplation and pure emotional experience. Rothko claimed that many people broke down and cried in front of his paintings. He explained, "The people who weep before my pictures are having the same religious experience as I had when I painted them."

Although de Kooning's *Woman* paintings are not straightforward depictions, they do reward the viewer who tries to figure out what the lines and shapes might represent. In *Woman I* (1950–52), the figure appears to be sitting on a grassy hill with her feet dangling in water. But there is no attempt at creating a sense of receding depth or volume through the use of perspective and shading. The *Woman* series, de Kooning said, "did one thing for me: it eliminated composition, arrangement, relationships, light." Women have

Still considered by many to be the greatest American architect of all time, Wright found inspiration for his building designs in the natural world. His theory of "organic architecture," or the idea that all elements of a building should be in harmony, had a decided influence on many architects who followed.

Ordinary objects serve as the starting point for Claes Oldenburg's large-scale sculptures, such as the steel *Clothespin* (1976), which stands 45 feet (13.7 m) high in downtown Philadelphia. Oldenburg creates his sculptures based on their surroundings and believes that each becomes "an emblem of its particular place."

been painted countless times in the course of art history, but they were often used as symbols for something else rather than representations of themselves. For de Kooning, the female figure had become an empty symbol; painting women was as liberating as pure abstraction.

Jasper Johns delighted in painting objects that had become so familiar as to almost lose their existence as objects, becoming—like de Kooning's women—empty symbols that are essentially abstract. *Flag* (1954–55) was the first of a series of paintings that Johns began in 1954, inspired by a dream he had about painting an American flag. The flag occupies the entire painting, eliminating any space between the object and the viewer and blurring the distinction between the object depicted and the object itself. At the same time, Johns made no attempt to hide his thick, obvious brushstrokes. He used newspaper dipped in colored wax to build up the surface under the paint, creating a rough appearance that gave it the feeling of a three-dimensional object, but also ensured that it could not be mistaken for "the real thing."

An exhibition called *The Store* (1961–62) by artist Claes Oldenburg (1929–) relied on a similarly ambiguous and playful treatment of the relationship between objects and their depictions. Oldenburg filled a storefront in a working-class neighborhood of New York with plaster sculptures of objects such as hamburgers, candy bars, underwear, and furniture. Because the pieces were all for sale, it was difficult to say whether they were merchandise or art depicting merchandise. The exhibition questioned distinctions between viewers in an art gallery and shoppers in a department store. Ironically, *The Store* later moved to an uptown gallery, embraced by the glitzy art world whose commercialization Oldenburg meant to criticize.

THE CIVIL RIGHTS MOVEMENT

After the Civil War and the abolition of slavery, racist laws were passed throughout the American South to perpetuate racial inequality. The civil rights movement challenged this system of repression, beginning in 1954 when the Supreme Court ruled in *Brown v. Board of Education* that separate facilities for black people violated the constitutional right to equality. In 1955, Rosa Parks refused to sit in the back of a Montgomery, Alabama, bus, where "colored" people were supposed to sit. In 1957, a group of black students bravely confronted soldiers who blocked their way into a Little Rock, Arkansas, high school. All over the country, ordinary people rose up in peaceful protest to claim their right to equality.

Lichtenstein began to draw on commercial art in his work partly as a result of his contact with Oldenburg. His comic book paintings were often copied from scenes in actual comics, with only slight alterations. In *Image Duplicator* (1963), he centralized the composition and added a helmet to frame the subject's face. A speech bubble asks, "What do you know about my image duplicator?" In the context of the painting, the question becomes a joke about the artist and his methods. Lichtenstein's paintings often made tongue-in-cheek references to their creator or themselves. The fact that the meaning of the comic book images changed when Lichtenstein transformed them into paintings suggests something about the power of art. By simply hanging them on the wall of a gallery, the transitory, meaningless images often became ironic commentaries on American life, art, and culture.

The Campbell's soup can was a commonplace object that people were used to seeing everywhere—except on the wall of an art gallery or museum. *Big Torn Campbell's Soup Can (vegetable beef)* (1962) is one of more than 30 paintings Warhol made of Campbell's soup cans. Americans were adjusting to being confronted daily by thousands of mass-produced images, and he was fascinated by the effect this had on art and perception. He wondered what would happen if he put a can of soup in an art gallery. He tried many variations, such as *200 Campbell's Soup Cans* (1962), in which many cans are depicted at once. They appear to be the same, but closer inspection reveals different types of soup and subtle changes in color. Warhol used images of movie stars such as Marilyn Monroe in similar ways, inviting comparison between factory-produced consumer goods and celebrity icons.

In his comic book-inspired paintings, such as *Reverie* (1965), Roy Lichtenstein used bold outlines and a narrow range of colors to imitate the comic book style. The defining characteristic of these pieces is the dots Lichtenstein placed among areas of color to imitate the technique used to add tone to mechanically reproduced artwork.

U.S. involvement in the Vietnam War lasted two decades, sparking many antiwar protests—some peaceful, some violent—in major cities and on college campuses throughout the country. By the end of the war, more than 50,000 American soldiers had been killed in combat.

Oldenburg's interest in the everyday items of pop culture can be seen in this untitled painting of a hamburger from 1961. The next year, the artist created a bed-sized canvas sculpture of a hamburger.

THE ARRIVAL OF POST-MODERNISM

Although Pop Art billed itself as art that bridged the gap to real life, in many ways it participated in the **escapism** that Americans embraced during the 1960s. Shopping and popular entertainment provided a welcome distraction from troubling events. The nuclear standoff of the Cold War continued to heighten anxiety, nearly erupting in 1962 when the U.S.S.R. installed missiles in Cuba. U.S. intervention in a civil war between Communist and democratic factions in Vietnam

escalated into a bloody, embarrassing war beginning in 1965, while at home, antiwar protests threatened to tear the nation apart. The civil rights movement that had begun in the 1950s also rocked the nation with protests, violence, and hatred born of prejudice. The assassinations of President John F. Kennedy and civil rights leader Martin Luther King Jr. in 1963 and 1968, respectively, shocked and grieved the nation. And a contentious new wave of the feminist movement brought a note of discord into every home, as wives and daughters rebelled against their traditional roles.

It was not until the booming postwar economy took a turn for the worse in the early 1970s that the psychological toll of these events finally caught up with American culture. American confidence, so high after World War

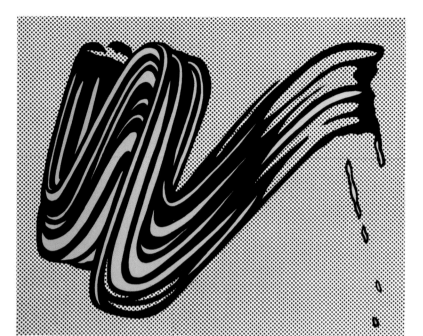

Unlike Pop Art images such as Lichtenstein's *Brushstroke* (1965, above), minimalist pieces such as Richard Serra's *Shovel Plate Prop* (1969, opposite) did not attempt to represent an object. Instead, they explored the properties of materials such as lead and reduced art to the minimum number of colors, shapes, lines, and textures.

II, sunk to a new low after an embarrassing withdrawal from Vietnam in 1973, and the Watergate scandal that led to President Richard Nixon's resignation in 1974 contributed to the general disillusionment. Even the relative success of the civil rights and feminist movements left many people feeling disoriented. The things they had valued, such as American democracy and the traditional family structure, could no longer be trusted. The world was not so black and white as it once seemed; there were only shades of gray. The Post-Modern era had begun.

The Modernist idea that art had to adapt to a changing world meant that the history of art was viewed as one long, linear progression. But such a narrow, centralized view of art history excluded art that fell outside the mainstream. Post-Modern artists believe that every form of culture is equally valuable. When historians attempt to make sense of the chaos of history by organizing it into neat chronological movements, they must make choices about what gets left out and what gets emphasized. Equality and openness to all forms of culture are sacrificed. Artists in the 1970s and '80s were intent on breaking down any structure or restrictive ideas that would obstruct and constrict art.

A Post-Modern movement known as Minimalism that flourished during the 1960s and '70s explored the farthest limits of what constituted art, eliminating not only references to the outside world, as Abstract Expressionism had done, but also the individuality and personal expression of the artist. Minimalist sculptures were simple, geometric shapes made of unfinished industrial materials such as fiberglass, plastic, aluminum, or wood.

Their simplicity resembled the paintings of Mark Rothko and a few other Abstract Expressionist painters, but the artists made no attempt at spiritual or emotional content. Post-Modernists recognized that everyone has a different viewpoint, and no one viewpoint is more correct than any other, so it is useless to make art that is supposed to mean any one thing. Art will mean whatever people interpret it to mean.

Other movements were more overtly political; they tried to balance things out by expressing viewpoints that had previously been ignored. Feminist Art, Black Art, and similar movements that began in the late 1960s brought artists who had previously been excluded from mainstream art to the forefront, challenging one-sided interpretations of history. These artists often used Pop Art techniques to depict and undermine racial and gender stereotypes. For example, in Robert Colescott's *George Washington Carver Crossing the Delaware* (1975), Aunt Jemima, Uncle Ben, and other stereotyped black characters parody a scene from American history that is depicted in gaudy colors and flattened shapes.

A side effect of the Post-Modernist position that nothing could be seen as more valuable or important than anything else was that nothing could be taken too seriously. For many artists, the tongue-in-cheek irony that was characteristic of Pop Art struck just the right note of intellectual playfulness. For example, the work of Conceptual artist Joseph Kosuth (1945–) consisted of enlarged dictionary entries, hung next to the objects they described. The Conceptual Art movement of the early 1970s rejected the idea that art is defined by the process of creation or the final product that results. Instead, artists focused on the idea behind a work of art. Conceptual art was often

Inspired by the modern world, Korean-born artist Nam June Paik uses pieces such as *Double Sided Arch* to question our preconceived ideas about television. In this sculpture constructed of TV sets, Paik uses both the positions of the TVs and the images on their screens to create his desired effect.

Taking his cue from an early fascination with nature, Robert Smithson created several massive earthworks, including *Spiral Jetty*, using natural materials. While most of his earthworks have been absorbed back into nature, this 15-foot-wide (4.5 m), 1,500-foot-long (457 m) spiral is still visible when water levels are low.

nearly unrecognizable as art, making it difficult for the general public to understand and enjoy.

Taking their cue from the "happenings" of Late Modernism, Post-Modern artists continued to break down barriers between art and life by creating art outside of museums and galleries. American artist Robert Smithson (1938–73) built a spiral-shaped wall of mud and rocks that extended into Utah's Great Salt Lake in *Spiral Jetty* (1970), and French artist Christo (1935–) wrapped 11 islands off the coast of Florida with pink fabric in *Surrounded Islands* (1980–83). Such works literally made art part of the world. Other artists pushed the boundaries of art by incorporating new media, such as video and the Internet. They often combined various media in one piece, defying traditional categories. For example, in the performance piece *TV-Cello* (1971) by Nam June Paik, a musician played a cello-like instrument that incorporated three TV monitors on which images changed to accompany the sounds.

Late Modernist art was now part of the established system of ideas against which artists launched their attacks. Nonetheless, artists continued to be influenced by it and to build on its innovations even as they criticized it. Post-Modern methods, such as performance art and **assemblage**, and themes, such as alienation, irony, and rebellion, were derived from the work of Late Modern artists. The most visible legacy of Late Modernism is the inevitable controversy, shock, and outrage that accompanies each new breakthrough in art. Although new styles and ideas have been rejected or ridiculed throughout art history, during the 20th century, the ability to evoke such reactions seemed to become a prerequisite for any new art to be taken seriously. Artists have pushed the envelope farther and farther in their quest to do something new and different.

Even in the works of a single artist such as Ed Ruscha, the style of Late Modernism manifested itself in many forms, from the typographical *OOF* (1962–63, opposite) to the commercial-looking *Standard Station* (1966, below).

There were repeated cries that "art is dead" throughout the 20th century—whether because the latest art was so new and different that people refused to accept that it was art, because artists despaired at ever being able to do something that had not been done before, or because artists feared that the world and the human race had changed so much that art could not possibly continue to be relevant. Despite these fears, art is not dead yet. Through the intense emotions of Pollock's *Autumn Rhythm*, the wry humor of Warhol's *Campbell's Soup Cans*, and a thousand other masterpieces, Late Modern art reaches across the years to inspire a new generation of artists and art-lovers.

TIMELINE

1945	Germany and Japan surrender to the Allies, ending World War II
1948	Jackson Pollock and Willem de Kooning hold their first one-man shows
1949	*Life* magazine profiles Pollock, proclaiming a new movement in American art
1950	Pollock paints *Autumn Rhythm: Number 30*
	Senator Joseph McCarthy launches his Communist witch hunt
1951	Mark Rothko paints *Untitled*
1952	De Kooning completes *Woman I*, the first painting in his *Woman* series
1954	The U.S. Supreme Court orders desegregation of schools in *Brown v. Board of Education*
1955	Jasper Johns completes *Flag*
	Rosa Parks refuses to sit in the back of an Alabama bus
1956	Eero Saarinen begins the TWA Terminal at New York's John F. Kennedy Airport
	Pollock is killed in a car accident
1957	Novelist Jack Kerouac writes the Beat classic *On the Road*
1958	Johns and Robert Rauschenberg hold their first one-man shows
1959	Frank Lloyd Wright completes the Solomon R. Guggenheim Museum in New York
1960	Jean Tinguely sets fire to *Homage to New York* before an invited audience
1961	Claes Oldenburg opens *The Store*
1962	Andy Warhol paints *Big Torn Campbell's Soup Can (vegetable beef)* and *200 Campbell's Soup Cans*
	Lichtenstein holds his first one-man show
1963	Lichtenstein paints *Image Duplicator*
	President John F. Kennedy is assassinated
1965	U.S. troops begin fighting in Vietnam
1966	Allen Kaprow coordinates *GAS*
1968	Martin Luther King Jr. is assassinated
1973	U.S. withdraws from Vietnam

GLOSSARY

abstract	a style of art that does not depict reality
assemblage	a form of art involving the arrangement of unrelated objects
collages	works of art made with pieces of a variety of materials, such as newspaper, photographs, and fabric
commercialization	the process of becoming focused on making money, especially when other values are sacrificed
Communist	espousing a system in which all property is owned by the community as a whole
controversial	causing disagreements and strong, opposing opinions
critics	people whose job is to form and express opinions and judgments about art
economy	a system of producing, distributing, and consuming wealth
escapism	the desire to escape from reality and its responsibilities
galleries	establishments for showing and selling works of art
Holocaust	the systematic murder of more than six million Jews and other Europeans by the Nazis, before and during World War II
ironic	humorous because of the contrast between what is expressed and what is meant
misogynist	hating, disliking, or distrusting women
one-man show	an exhibition at a gallery in which all of the works are by one artist
propaganda	the systematic, widespread promotion of particular ideas and doctrines, often in a distorted or deceptive manner
silk-screening	a method of printing in which ink, paint, or dye is pressed through a silk-covered stencil, creating a smooth, clean appearance
stencils	sheets of solid material with letters or designs cut out so that when ink or paint is applied they are marked on the surface beneath
studio	a room in which an artist works
U.S.S.R.	Union of Soviet Socialist Republics; a Communist nation in Eastern Europe and northern Asia, formerly part of the Russian empire, that existed between 1917 and 1991

INDEX